26/6 - 92

For Gerard
with lot of love

Kim

D1614865

A NECKLACE OF BEES

OSIP MANDELSTAM

A NECKLACE OF BEES

Selected Poems

Translated by Maria Enzensberger
Foreword and Afterword by
Elaine Feinstein

MENARD/KING'S

1992

A Necklace of Bees:
Poems by Osip Mandelstam

Translations © 1992: The Estate of Maria Enzensberger

Cover design by Merlin James

Distribution in North America by SPD Inc
1814 San Pablo Avenue
Berkeley, Cal 94702   USA

ISBN 0 9513753 6 9

The Menard Press
8 The Oaks
Woodside Avenue
London N12 8AR
081-446-5571

King's College London
c/o Adam Archive Publications
Strand
London
WC2R 2LS

Typeset by Wendy Pank
Book production by Fakenham Photosetting Limited

ELAINE FEINSTEIN

FOREWORD

Osip Mandelstam is one of this century's literary martyrs. Through his wife Nadezhda's brilliant memoir, more readers learnt of his reckless poem about Stalin, his subsequent harassment, and his final disappearance in the Vladivostok transit camp in 1938, than could hope to have any direct response to the poems which made him at once memorable and dangerous. Yet Mandelstam's love of poetry was closely bound up with his love of this world; which is why, as Sinyavsky long ago observed, Mandelstam never stopped finding a meaning in it. His letters are touched with a poignant, resilient optimism to the last.

Maria Enzensberger has chosen not only early poems where Mandelstam is grateful for the quiet joy of being alive, but later poems which have the flavour of smoke and grief'; the abrupt, intimate, miraculous poems of Mandelstam's years in exile. And here these translations speak with heart-breaking clarity, as Mandelstam knocks deliriously on 'his wooden box' to beg deliriously for a reader or 'at least someone to talk to on the staircase'; and his voice calls with unbearable loneliness from his five days train journey to Siberia:

'If only I could have an inch of blue sea
just a needle's eye full'

TRANSLATOR'S ACKNOWLEDGEMENTS

I am grateful to the following for their help in the
preparation of this volume:
Elaine and Arnold Feinstein, Gessy Gathercole,
James Greene, Jo Labanyi, Elizabeth Millar and
Cathy Porter.
I also want to thank my brother, Mikhail Fadeyev,
for providing photographs of Mandelstam.

(Publisher's p.s.: The figures in the double page
photograph are, from left to right, O. Mandelstam,
K. Chukowsky, B. Lifshitz, Y. Annenkopf.)

NOTE ON THE TEXT

The Russian text and the numbering of
Mandelstam's poems in the list of contents come
from his *Sobranie sochineniy* (Collected Works),
Vol 1 (2nd ed., revised and expanded, 1967), ed.
Gleb Struve and Boris Filippov, with introductions
by Clarence Brown, Gleb Struve and E.M. Rais,
Published by New York. Inter-Language Literary
Associates. Most of the poems are untitled.

PUBLISHER'S NOTE

I discussed Masha Enzensberger's translations
with her before she died and she agreed to a few
proposed changes. We were to have had a final
session before going to press. In the circumstances
I have decided to make a few additional minor
changes which I am confident she would have
agreed to.

A.R.
3 January 1992

The translator dedicates this work to the memory of her sister, the poet Tatyana Makarova.

CONTENTS

Foreword by Elaine Feinstein 5
Acknowledgements 6
Note on the Text 6

POEMS

I am blessed with a body – what shall I do with it
(from *Stone*, 8) 11

Where the noisy glass of a torrent
(published posthumously, 149) 12

O sky, o sky, I'll dream about you!
(from *Stone*, 27) 13

A new moon in the azure
(published posthumously, 155) 14

Hiding inside my own self like a serpent
(published posthumously, 162) 15

'Here I stand – I can do no other'
(from *Stone*, 43) 16

Kinematograph
(from *Stone*, 50) 17

Dombey & Son
(from *Stone*, 53) 19

The State dramatically premature
(published posthumously, 190) 20

O the smell of poplars! Drunk
(published posthumously, 191) 21

Take from my palms, for your delight and joy
(from *Tristia*, 116) 22

Can't remember how long
(from *Poems*, 131) 23

To no one should you tell
(published posthumously, 201) 24

Help me, Lord, to survive this night
(published posthumously, 223) 25

For the thundering glory of years to come
(published posthumously, 227) 26

Preserve my words
(published posthumously, 235) 27

Excerpts from destroyed poems
(published posthumously, 237-238) 28

I am no patriarch yet
(published posthumously, 251) 29

As water running from a single mountain crack
(published posthumously, 287) 31

The day was rearing its five heads. For five
(published posthumously, 313) 32

I shall wonder at the world a little bit longer
(published posthumously, 323) 34

O where am I to throw myself this January?
(published posthumously, 360) 35

Armed with the eyesight of the slender wasps
(published posthumously, 367) 36

There were two eyes sharper than scythes
(published posthumously, 368) 37

I shall say this provisionally – whispering
(published posthumously, 376) 38

Charlie Chaplin
(published posthumously, 386) 39

The translator 41

Afterword by Elaine Feinstein 42

I am blessed with a body - what shall I do with it,
All of a piece and so much my own?

To whom, tell me, should I be grateful for
The quiet joy of being alive and breathing?

I am the gardener, and the flower too;
I'm not abandoned in the world's dungeon.

My breathing has already left a trace
Upon eternity's untarnished window panes.

The pattern that will linger on, ingrained,
Has been unrecognisable of late.

The moment's drizzle may trickle down the panes,
The cherished pattern cannot be effaced.

1909

Where the noisy glass of a torrent
Bursts out of captivity,
The swirling foam
Hardens like a swan's wing.

O time, do not torment with envy
Him who became congealed at the right moment:
We have been raised by the foam of chance
And joined together by its lace.

O sky, o sky, I'll dream about you!
You can't have gone completely blind;
The day's burnt out like a white page,
Leaving some smoke and a bit of ash behind.

1911

A new moon in the azure
Is clear and bright,
On the road, a horseshoe
Is testing the ground.

I sighed deeply –
The sky was blue –
As if drawing water
 With a silver spoon.

I put on a heavy
Crown of happiness,
A blacksmith is merrily
Forging and hammering.

1911

Hiding inside my own self like a serpent,
Twining around myself like an ivy,
I rise above myself.

I want myself, I fly towards myself,
Splashing water
With dark outstretched wings.

Like a startled eagle who, on return,
Fails to find his nest,
Fallen into an abyss.

I'll rinse myself with the fire of lightning
And, entreating the heavy thunder,
Vanish into a cold cloud.

1912

'Hier stehe ich — ich kann nicht anders'

Here I stand - I can do no other,
A mountain made dark will never change its
  colour,
And Luther's spirit, sinister and stark,
Is hovering above St. Peter's spire.

1913

KINEMATOGRAPH

Kinematograph. Three benches.
A sentimental fever rises.
A rich aristocratic lady
Entangled by a wicked rival.

You cannot stop the flight of passion:
She isn't to blame for her enslavement,
Innocently, like a sister,
She fell in love with a naval officer.

The bastard-son of a grey— haired count,
He seeks his fortune in the desert.
Heart-rending flows the account
Of the lovers' torment and estrangement.

And frantically, like a gipsy,
She wrings her hands in deep despair.
She is abandoned. Music screeches
From an exhausted ancient piano.

Her heart, ingenuous and helpless,
Summons up its last resources:
She steals the most important papers
Sought by enemy headquarters.

A monstrous motor car is speeding
Along an empty chestnut alley.
The film is chirping, hearts are beating,
Astounded, alarmed and happy.

In simple clothes, with a briefcase,
She travels in a train compartment,
Consumed and haunted by her fears,
Yet beautiful and unrecanting.

O what a cruel flight of fancy:
The end does not justify the means!
For him – the title and inheritance,
For her – a rueful life in prison.

1913

DOMBEY & SON

When I hear – shriller than a whistle
The sound of the English language,
I remember Oliver Twist
Surrounded by piles of ledgers.

You may discover from Dickens
The London of those days:
The firm of Dombey in the City,
The yellow water in the Thames.

Long rains and tears. Fairhaired
And gentle boy – Dombey the son.
He is the only one there
Who does not grasp the biting puns.

The broken chairs in the office,
The pence and shillings added up,
Like bees, the buzzing sums are swarming,
Like hornets, poisonous and sharp.

The mortal sting of the attorneys
Has pierced the tobacco loops,
And like a dampened piece of clothing,
The bankrupt dangles in the noose.

Condemned and ruined by the lawyers,
He won't be salvaged by laments.
Abondoned, crying inconsolably,
His daughter clasps his chequered pants.

1913

The State dramatically premature
The earth laments –
We all shall join a long black queue
In the black square of the Kremlin.

O the smell of poplars! Drunk
With the feeling that the world is ending,
We are the trouble-makers – not for trouble's sake –
In the black square of the Kremlin.

The waxen faces of cathedrals
Sleep solemnly. Untamed,
Ivan the Great [1] – the lonely brigand –
Like a gallows is wild and straight.

1917

---

[1]. A Kremlin belfry.

Take from my palms, for your delight and joy,
A little honey and a little sun,
As Persephone's bees commanded.

The punt unmoored cannot be untied,
The furry shadows cannot be discerned,
Nor life's incessant terror surmounted.

What's left to us, is only a kiss –
The kisses bristly like the little bees
That die the moment they desert the hive.

They rustle in night's transparent jungles,
Living on time, meadowsweet and mint –
The children of the forest of Taigetos.

Take for your joy my present, simple and wild –
Uncomely, shrivelled necklace
Of bees that died transforming honey into sun.

November 1920

Can't remember how long
This song's been known to me –
Does a thief slink along to its tune
Or the prince of mosquitoes drone?

I would like just one more time
To speak of nothing at all,
To blaze up like a match in the dark,
Or nudge night awake with my shoulder.

To lift off the air's hat
Like a smothering haystack,
To shake up a heavy sack
Chock-full of caraway seeds.

So that the flow of blood
And the ringing of dry grass
Ever after would ripple on
Through the ages, the hayloft, the dream.

1922

To no one should you tell
What you have seen. Forget
The bird, the old woman, the jail
And all the rest.

Or else, as you start to speak,
When the day begins,
Shudders sharp as pine needles
Will prickle your skin.

You'll remember the summer wasp,
Pencil case stained with ink
Or blueberries in the forest
You never bothered to pick.

Tiflis, October 1930

Help me, Lord, to survive this night.
It's my life – your slave – I fear for.
Living in Petersburg is like sleeping in a coffin.

1931

For the thundering glory of years to come,
For the valiant tribe of men,
I've relinquished the cup at the elders' repast
And my gaiety, honour and grace.

Our wolfhound age digs its teeth in my neck,
But I am no wolf in my blood,
Better stuff me away like a hat in the sleeve
Of the shaggy Siberian steppe.

So that I would see no coward or mud,
No bloody remains on the wheel,
So that, every night, foxes glowed for me,
Dazzling in their silver attire.

Take me into the night where the Yenisey flows
And the pine-trees reach out to the stars,
For, you know, I am no wolf in my blood,
Me — no one but an equal destroys.

1931

To Anna Akhmatova

P reserve my words
     for their flavour of smoke and grief,
Their resin of patience
     and conscientious tar of labour.
That's the way water gleams in a Novgorod well,
     black and sweet,
To reflect seven fins of the star
     that ascends every Christmas.
In return, father, friend,
     my rough-handed helpmate,
I – the brother rejected,
     the human family's worst outcast –
Promise that I shall build wooden wells
     so fearsome
That the Tartars could lower princes in tubs
     for a torturous bath.
Only make those old executioner's blocks
     love me forever!
Like the players at skittles who, aiming at death,
     hit nine pins,
To achieve this, I'll walk all my life
     in a robe of iron
And will find in a forest a solid axe-handle
     that ancient beheading demands.

Khmelnitskaya, 13 May 1931

I

In the thirty first year of this century,
I returned, no, read: was returned
By force to Buddhist Moscow. Before that, though,
I managed to see Ararat
Graced with its Biblical tablecloth.
I spent two hundred days in the land of
Eternal Sabbaths called Armenia.
When you are thirsty there, they give you water
From the Kurdish spring Arzni –
Good, prickly, dry and most truthful water.

II

I've now grown fond of Moscow ways
And don't miss Arzni water any longer.
In Moscow, there are bird-cherry trees
And telephones and ...

I am no patriarch yet,
But still of semivenerable age:
People still scold me in the language
Of a tram squabble – 'You so and so!...'
Well, I apologize,
But deep down, I do not change...

As you reflect on your connection with the world,
You don't believe yourself — it's all nonsense!
A midnight key to someone else's flat,
A twenty-copeck coin in your pocket,
A bit of celluloid – a gangster film.

I rush to the telephone like a puppy
To answer every anxious ringing voice.
It offers me in Polish – 'Dziekue panu' –
An outlandish gracious reproach,
Or else a promise that will not be honoured.

You wonder – what should you take a fancy to?
Caught amidst squibs and firecrackers,
You boil over but regain your temper. So what is left?
Not much – turmoil and unemployment.
Well, those won't give you a light, will they?

I smile wryly, then timidly assume
An air of dignity. Off I go for a walk
With a blonde cane –
I listen to sonatas in the streets
And lick my lips at every vendor's stall,
Leaf books in stone gateways:
I do not live and yet I am alive.

I'll turn my steps toward sparrows
Or reporters, or street photographers:
Within five minutes a little shovel
Will lift out of a tiny tray my image
Under the cone of the lilac mountain, Shah.

Or else I'll dive into steamy cellars
Where neat and honest Chinese cooks
Pick up batter balls with chopsticks,
Play narrow cards and drink vodka
Like swallows from the river Kiang.

I like the clattering trams at the junction
And the Astrakhan caviare of asphalt
Spread with straw mats like Spumante baskets;
And the ostrich plumage
Of Lenin's building sites.

I enter the marvellous lairs of museums
Where monster-Rembrandts goggle,
Rivalling the lustre of Cordovan leather.
I wonder at Titian's horned mitres
And at multi-coloured Tintorettos
Garish as a thousand parrots.

How I long to become talkative, playful,
To speak the truth,
To send melancholy to hell, to the quagmire,
Take someone by the hand and say:
'Be gentle, we are going the same way...'

Moscow, July - September 1931

As water running from a single mountain crack
Is contradictory: two faced –
Half hard, half soft, half sweet, half bitter.

So to die completely,
I must first forfeit – a thousand times a day –
Sigh's freedom and a sense of purpose.

Moscow, December 1933

31

The day was rearing its five heads. For five
      long days and nights, [1]
Shrinking, I was taking pride in the space
      that spread around like dough.
Sleep was older than hearing, hearing older than sleep –
      keen and solid.
Roads careered, chasing us
      in a coachman's race.
The day was rearing its five heads. Mad
      from this dance,
Mounted men went on riding,
      the black mass trudged along.
The expansion of power's aorta
      through white nights, no – knives –
Turned eyes into coniferous flesh.
If only I could have an inch of blue sea,
      just a needle's eye full ...
To enable the escort of time to sail smoothly.
Russian fairy tale – humble meal. Wooden spoon.
      Haloo!
Where are you, the three lovely lads
      from the iron gate of the GPU? [2]
To make sure Pushkin's marvellous goods
      did not pass into parasites' hands
A tribe of Pushkin scholars –
      in overcoats and with guns –
Is getting its schooling

– Young lovers of whitetoothed rhymes,
If only I could have an inch of blue sea,
    just a needle's eye full ...
The train was speeding towards the Urals.
    Out of a sound movie,
Chapayev[3] was riding into our open mouths
    to die
Behind a wooden stockade on a white sheet, die
    and jump onto his horse.

1935

---

[1] The poem describes Mandelstam's journey to Siberia.
[2] The acronym of the Chief Political Administration – the
    successor to the Cheka and the predecessor of the KGB.
[3] A Civil War hero and the eponymous protagonist of a
    popular film.

I shall wonder at the world a little bit longer:
At children, at snow,
But a smile is incorruptible like a road,
Disobedient, not a servant.

1936

O where am I to throw myself this January?
The open city's maddeningly tenacious ...
Or have I become drunk on closed doors?
All locks and catches make me want to roar.

The stockings of the barking alleyways,
The creaking store-rooms of the knotted lanes,
The cellar freaks scuttle into their quarters
And hastily emerge from them again.

I skid into a dark and warty pit,
Sliding towards an icy water-tower
And, stumbling, munch the January sleet
And startle the rooks into a fevered flutter.

I follow them, groaning, I knock
On some wooden box in a delirious haze:
'O please, a reader! a well-wisher! doctor! —
Someone to talk to on the staircase!'

Voronezh, end of January / February 1936

Armed with the eyesight of the slender wasps
That sip and suckle on the earth's axis,
I sense all I have witnessed in the past
And recollect it easily and painlessly.

I neither sing, nor draw, nor wield a bow,
The black-voiced bow of a slim viola,
I only bite into life's core
And love to envy wasps, astute and boisterous.

If only some day – deflecting sleep and death –
A goad of air and sun-light tangles
Could make me hear in its timeless strength
The stubborn drone of the earth's axis.

1937

36

There were two eyes sharper than scythes,
A cuckoo in each pupil and a drop of dew.

They were barely able – grown full size –
To distinguish the lonely constellations of stars.

1937

I shall say this provisionally – whispering,
It's too early to say it yet:
What we see as the sky's playful mystery
Is achieved through experience and sweat.

Under the transient sky of purgatory,
We hardly remember at all –
The sky is a happy sanctuary,
A lifelong, extendible home.

Voronezh, 9 March 1937

Charlie Chaplin
           Stepped out of the cinema,
Two soles,
           A harelip,
Two peepers
           Full of ink
And of fine astonished energy.
Charlie Chaplin –
           A harelip,
Two soles –
           A wretched fate.
Something is the matter with the way we all live.
           Strangers, strangers.
Pewter horror
           On his face,
The head
           Wouldn't hold up,
Soot is walking,
           Shoe polish is mincing,
And softly-softly
           Chaplin says:
What's the point
           Of my being cherished and loved,
           Even celebrated?
And a big highroad takes him to
           Strangers, strangers.
Charlie Chaplin,
           Press upon the pedal,
Charlie, rabbit,
           Break into your role,

Peel blood-oranges,

              Put on your roller-skates.

Your wife

      Is a blind shadow,

And the foreign land ahead ever unpredictable.

Why is it

      That Chaplin has a tulip?

Why

   Is the crowd so friendly?

Because this,

      After all, is Moscow.

Charlie, Charlie,

         You must take risks,

This is no time to get dispirited.

Your bowler hat

        Is but another ocean,

And Moscow is so close

           That one feels bewitched

           By the beckoning road.

                          1937

ELAINE FEINSTEIN

AFTERWORD

My husband and I saw Masha last September in
Moscow a few weeks before she died. She seemed
then both animated and gay; she had been on the
barricades resisting the putsch, and looked almost
as she had when we first made friends. Sometimes
I think of her now at the centre of one of her
parties, presiding over a brightly-coloured table of
Russian delicacies, and commanding the toasts.
Mainly, I remember her voice. Masha was the
true voice of Russian poetry for me from the first
day she read the poems of Tsvetayeva aloud at my
request more than twenty years ago. I shall
always miss her intuitive understanding and the
warmth of her friendship.

THE TRANSLATOR:

Maria Enzensberger was born in Moscow, the daughter of a famous Soviet poet Margarita Aliger. She read English at Moscow University. Having married the German poet and essayist Hans Magnus Enzensberger, she left the Soviet Union in 1967 and lived in the United States, Cuba and Germany before coming to Britain in 1969. She made this country her permanent home while always maintaining close links with her native Russia. She was one of the first women fellows of King's College, Cambridge, 1972-1976, doing research in the Russian avant-garde arts and literature of the first decades of this century. Maria Enzensberger taught Film Studies at Staffordshire Polytechnic, the Polytechnic of Central London and the University of Warwick. In 1987, she published her translations of Vladimir Mayakovsky,*Listen!*, (The Redstone Press), which were read at the National Theatre, the ICA and the Serpentine Gallery.

Maria Enzensberger was born in 1943. She died in 1991. The reader is referred to Neal Ascherson's moving and eloquent obituary in *The Independent* of October 16, 1991.